Pelican Tracks

CRAB ORCHARD AWARD SERIES IN POETRY

Pelican Tracks

Elton Glaser

Crab Orchard Review

& Southern Illinois University Press

CARBONDALE AND EDWARDSVILLE

06   05   04   03   4   3   2   1

The Crab Orchard Award Series in Poetry is a joint publishing
venture of Southern Illinois University Press and *Crab Orchard Review.*
This series has been made possible by the generous support of the
Office of the President of Southern Illinois University and the
Office of the Vice Chancellor for Academic Affairs and Provost
at Southern Illinois University Carbondale.

Crab Orchard Award Series in Poetry Editor: Jon Tribble
Judge for 2002: Tim Seibles

Library of Congress Cataloging-in-Publication Data

Glaser, Elton.
    Pelican tracks / Elton Glaser.
       p. cm. — (Crab Orchard award series in poetry)
    I. Title. II. Series.
    PS3557.L314 P38 2003
    811'.54—dc21
    ISBN 0-8093-2516-0 (pbk. : alk. paper)   2002010913

Printed on recycled paper. ♻

The paper used in this publication meets the minimum
requirements of American National Standard for Information
Sciences—Permanence of Paper for Printed Library Materials,
ANSI Z39.48-1992. ∞

For Dan and Cyndie and Karen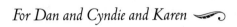

Contents

Acknowledgments ix

One

And Redeye Gravy with Everything 3
Solstice in Capricorn 4
Ohio Haiku 5
Immaterial Witness 7
Akron after a Spring Rain 9
Plus Shipping and Handling 10
Dead Reckoning 12
The Youngstown Breakfast Show 13
Alligator Pears 16
O Holy Night 17
Swampscape with Oil Platform 18
Living in OH 20
Metairie Cemetery 22
Drowning in Ohio 23
Incompatibles in the Wild Light 24

Two

1945 29
Mardi Gras Indians 30
Grand Isle 31
Bedtime Legends near Esplanade 33
Hurricane Lamp 35
Trailers 36
The Worst High School Marching Band in the South 38
Benjamin in the Salvage Yard 41
Problem Child 43
Late Fifties on Front Street 45
2 Drink Minimum 46
Evening Services on North Rampart Street 48
To John, in Alaska 50

Three
Storyville 55

Four
Time Zones 65
Shucking 66
Family Possessions 68
Pilgrimage 71
Louisiana Elegies 74
Listening to My Mother Breathe 76
Oscillating Fan 78
Elegy for Clifton Chenier 81
On My Mother's Death 83
Pelican Tracks in the Rain Dreaming 84
Black Baptist Funeral 85
Endsheet 88

Notes 91

Acknowledgments

I gratefully acknowledge the following magazines, in which many of these poems first appeared, some in slightly different versions:

Akron—"On My Mother's Death"

Alligator Juniper—"Alligator Pears," "Plus Shipping and Handling"

America—"Akron after a Spring Rain"

Borderlands—"Hurricane Lamp," "Shucking"

Clackamas Literary Review—"Incompatibles in the Wild Light"

Fine Madness—"Louisiana Elegies," "O Holy Night"

The Florida Review—"Mardi Gras Indians," "Solstice in Capricorn"

The Georgia Review—"Endsheet"

The Gettysburg Review—"Late Fifties on Front Street"

Indiana Review—"Storyville"

The Ledge—"And Redeye Gravy with Everything," "Listening to My Mother Breathe"

Louisiana Literature—"Bedtime Legends near Esplanade," "Black Baptist Funeral," "Family Possessions," "Ohio Haiku," "Pilgrimage"

Mid-American Review—"The Youngstown Breakfast Show"

Monster—"Pelican Tracks in the Rain Dreaming"

Parnassus—"The Worst High School Marching Band in the South"

The Plum Review—"Living in OH"

Poetry—"Time Zones"

Poetry Northwest—"Oscillating Fan"

Southern Humanities Review—"Grand Isle"

Southern Poetry Review—"Elegy for Clifton Chenier," "Trailers"

The Sow's Ear Poetry Review—"2 Drink Minimum"

"Evening Services on North Rampart Street" was published and "Pilgrimage" was reprinted in *Uncommonplace: An Anthology of Contemporary Louisiana Poets*, edited by Ann B. Dobie (Baton Rouge: Louisiana State University Press, 1998).

"Drowning in Ohio" was published and "Ohio Haiku" was reprinted in *I Have My Own Song for It: Modern Poems of Ohio*, edited by Elton Glaser and William Greenway (Akron: University of Akron Press, 2002).

"To John, in Alaska" won the 1995 Milton Dorfman Poetry Prize.

"2 Drink Minimum" won the 1996 poetry prize from *The Sow's Ear Poetry Review.*

"Solstice in Capricorn" was one of five poems that won the 1998 Editors' Award from *The Florida Review.*

"Plus Shipping and Handling" won the 1999 poetry prize from *Alligator Juniper.*

For fellowships that helped me to complete poems for this book, I would like to thank the University of Akron and the National Endowment for the Arts.

One

I am like a pelican of the wilderness. . . .

PSALM 102

And Redeye Gravy with Everything

Back in the Midwest, after the snowmad rise
Through the mountains of Kentucky, the tall trucks
Sucking past in a spume of delirious wheels,
The whole highway run amuck, wiper blades
Slaphappy at the streaks of salt and slop,
And ahead, two hundred tired miles to home.

We stop to gas up at a crossroads diner,
Tables of fat women buttering their chins, drivers
Hollow-eyed at the slippery end of the meal,
Skid marks of bacon, eggs sliding across the plate,
And crankcase coffee only the dead could drink—
An hour of sweet amnesia from the lethal road.

And we think, why come back to this winterbeaten state,
Whose motto must be *The bland leading the bland?*
There's not much call for okra in Akron, or crawfish in Kent,
Or pancakes paved with the blackstrap tar of molasses.
Even the border drawl from the hills has gone mute, extinct
As the Carolina parakeet and the carbonated warbler.

And why come back before the Ice Age retreats, a trip
That's close to steering down a long sleeve of silk,
The heater's breath like a small dog panting up your leg?
We pay the bill and scrape the windshield clean,
Still trembling from the tight grind of clutch and squint,
Knuckles so white they glow like raw bone.

Solstice in Capricorn

Darker days; that tragedy of trees
Widowed by the wind. North of north.

Come lie by me while the house aches.
Cold cracks its whip across my back.

What's so hard about love? It stays,
When worms go underground from the damp leaves.

Fifty years a witness to winter, but none
So crazed as this one, so close.

You nude on the blue bed; you
Warming the night's ice in your arms.

Starpoints; shock of a bruised moon.
Speed of blood in the bone marrow.

Words come with their own slow will.
I feel them freeze on the tongue.

Speak for me. Say that, even now,
In the seizure of my voice, something

Still stirs and flows. Say that for me,
In the heat you have in your keeping.

Ohio Haiku

1

Why did those pioneers, having come this far, decide
To stop? They must have known, by scout
Or second sight, that nothing lay ahead but Indiana.

2

Under this sudden embarrassment of snow, the last leaves lie
Plastered like a bald man's nightmare:
Little wet toupees stuck crooked on the skull.

3

The quaint pavements of Paris, the flagstone squares of Florence
Have their charm in tourist photographs, but we've got
The real slideshow here: the streets of Akron cobbled in ice.

4

I'm no scholar of politics, no minister of history,
But I believe what that good book said:
All the presidents nobody ever heard of came from Ohio.

5

That squirrel in the bird feeder, that pirate of seeds,
Why isn't he scrabbling on the front lawn,
A buccaneer of buckeyes and the lesser nuts?

6

Driving to Athens from the east, you must first go through
Guysville and Coolville, as if Plato's *Republic*
Were printed inside a comic book, in the hairy panels of R. Crumb.

7

If you know what the weeping cherry stands for, and why
The willow hangs its head in the wind,
Then how could you tap this maple for its sticky tears?

8

—Lake at the top end, river at the bottom, and both holding back
Those low fields, that flat middle the hills keep
Slipping down to, as if land, like water, seeks its own level.

9

Custer, that boy-general, native son of this state,
Sweetened his locks with oil of cinnamon.
Three days after he fell, you could still smell him on the dead slope.

10

Not okra, but corn; not crawfish, but pike;
No Fat Tuesday, but a full
Year of seven thin days to the week.

11

If Adam had been dusted off in Ohio, he and Eve would
Own a small orchard somewhere near Seville,
Selling, from their roadside stand, jugs of cider with a homely bite.

12

In this city too new for temples, too busy
To dig up a buried word or bone,
I lean on my own past, the only ruin still standing.

Immaterial Witness

Here's what I'm looking for, after the harvest
And the first encroachments of frost—

A moon whose fire
Won't burn through the broken atmosphere
But silvers the mist, my eye taking

Delight in light

That glows like a face of vapor,
A ghost in the glass,
Pale hands
Wiping the wet away, polishing the dark.

A few simple beautiful things—
When did I ever want
More than that?

But this is no bell for meditation,
No pillow for the dreaming head;
It's white, white as cocaine
With its cold clarities.

In the sweat of the bedroom window,
The moon lays down
A chalk outline of my body,

Half-erased, drifting
Like smoke from a smothered wick

(In Spain, they call the cup
That puts the candle out
The hand of Judas).

From the sleepy side of death,
The stars strike deep,
Double-daggers
On a chart marking the wrecks at sea.

Circle of salt,
It comes to testify
At the injured end of night,

Night soaked
In serums and alarms, the sheets
A poultice for parts unknown, gauze
Over the sticky damages.

Such ruins! Such small enormities!

When the mind's lost in midair
Like a sky in the private
Inertias of snow,

Who would presume to muse,
And on what? This moon,
Immaterial witness
In the tint of winter, remote
As the last thought that passed through me—

This moon won't melt
Even when the sun peels back
The frozen levels and the freezing seams,

But I will, a pool of
Blue impurities, hard water worn down,

In which a bird on its long flight south
Has landed for a drink, and soon
Lifts off again, taking some
Wasted share of me

Home on the tired tremor of its wings.

Akron after a Spring Rain

The air comes clean, stone-scrubbed and rough, a sea air
Without the salt. And the daffodils,
Their color blunt as butter substitute,
Bang their heads on the breeze—
Even Wordsworth can't ruin them for me now.

Look around. Everything's on the brink, or just beyond—
Dogwoods wet in their dark bark; big drops
Sliding from the fringe of evergreens;
Saucer magnolia deep in its cups;
A spasm of crabs, and maples sticky with foetal leaves.

All down the walkway, the bricks glistening, the day
Still chill enough to let me know
This is April in the Midwest,
I rub my tired sight
Against the sway of tulips, redheads sultry in the sun.

And then the rain again, racing over me, and gone—
Blue in the sudden pools, a thin river
Between my feet. The afternoon plays
Good cop, bad cop, till I confess
There's something I love even in this slippery spring.

Plus Shipping and Handling

I'm waiting to see if all these insights, these dark
residual visions of insomnia, will burn down to
vapor and ash that hour after dawn,

that hour when the drowsy sun pulls itself up
behind the luminous maples, each leaf
shining as if lit from within.

Already the grackles are out walking knock-kneed
over the lawn, like a flock of philosophers
who have laced both shoes together.

Already the dog next door, his howl halfway between
a wolf and a vacuum cleaner, is making me think
of sprinkling poison on the pork chops.

And those early strollers in their stretch pants, squares
circling the block, pace by again and again,
gazelles of polyester in the first light.

With my Buddha belly and my Confucian stoop,
I can face the east from either side of
that seesaw trauma of the soul,

at one end, crisis, at the other end, Christ,
as if I didn't have enough to do all day
solving the mysteries of the quotidian,

enigmas that leave me so weak I'll need each night
baling wire for the brain cells, and another
martini IV, olives flavoring the drip,

hex of the meat-haters, curse of the smoke-chokers,
who must have found some way to live forever
in pure fear of the flesh.

Deep in the farmlands, the good folks busy themselves,
up with the dew and the rooster, storing the hay,
stacking the canned corn in the root cellar.

And somewhere lovers are brushing the crumbs of wedding cake
from their sheets, mouthwash in the champagne glasses,
aspirin in the bride's pink hand.

Here, where the clocks conspire, and the church bells
certify the day like a notary public,
I'm wrapping my throat against

the cold gold of October, a new scarf of
Polynesian pinwheels woven in the wool,
to keep my voice warm for

crying out at any revelations on the sidewalk,
sudden epiphanies delivered by the fall
and paid for in pain at full price.

Dead Reckoning

I'm done with
The abundance of winter, so full of itself,
The air no more than snow
And the earth no less, nothing multiplied
Zero by zero, until
I can't take it, I can't
Keep my mind from skating away
Somewhere south, as the ice melts
To blue and green and a red-tailed hawk
Riding the air, broken summer
Of the sun's division, where the world
Comes back again, piece by piece,
And I see my shadow
Split the shore, walking the dark
Tideline between the beaten sand
And a thousand white arousals of the sea.

The Youngstown Breakfast Show

for William Greenway

Those things on the plate—
Do they have a name, not uptown or foreign,
But something sweaty and hard-earned,
Suitable for citizens whose last paycheck
Was split between
The guys at the Greasem and Rackem Garage
And the bartender at Bob's Bowlarama?
Or is it still
Too early in the morning to mention food, especially
If it's yellow and pulsing, or limp?
No, we've never seen bacon with varicose veins before,
Or eggs so addled
They can't lie still on the Melmac.

Let the camera
Turn somewhere else, anywhere else,
As the voice-over intones
The message of the day, so blurred and brief
No one can tell
Which god's been sidestepped
In this prayer of evasive action.

But no pictures of steel mills, please,
No pig iron at this hour, no
Rusty photographs of abandoned plants, the windows
Punched out like a boxer's lights.
If you're up by now,
You're already depressed, and it would be
Bad manners to rub it in.

Let's flash those grainy frames, the beef
Of the high school football team blown-up each Friday night,
For in football there is hope,
Never mind the mud or the score. We all like
That look of innocence in a hard helmet,
Taken just after the cheerleaders
Misspelled their mascot through the megaphones,
And two days before the grades came in.

O you can't be breezy enough, not when
You're too full of beans—
As our hosts must know, high spirits
On the Naugahyde, though their hands
Shake from a hundred cups of coffee
And the tension of trying to please
The shut-ins and insomniacs, the wives
Folding a sleepy piece of meat for the lunchbox.

He's landed here from a larger market,
The last stop before he works
Some cable show for call-in lovers with a nasty rash,
Or inflates the grand opening of a new department store
Where the fashions could trace themselves
To a blind designer and a pool of petroleum.
And she's from local stock,
Miss Gooseberry of 1992, a miracle of
Reconstructive wiring from teeth to tits. Don't ask
How she got this job: when the ad said *Vacancy*,
No one doubted she could fill the slot.

But it's all so much chatter, warm and harmless
Behind the hollow eyes and the hair
Built to withstand a shock of 8.2 on the Richter scale,
All an interlude of evanescence
Between the station breaks and the farm reports
And the spots our sponsors pay for:
Video hallucinations

Shot by a kid in a baseball cap, who's already
Failed his finals three times at film school, and who thinks
Movies lost their grip on the sacred after *Repo Man.*
If you can't afford a backlot on a Youngstown budget,
You can still find that
Sci-fi effect on the streets, the camera
Swooping and zooming and taking aim
In unnatural angles at the ordinary, the lens
Swollen with a crazed face
As the owner of Big Eddie's Body Shop
Pitches his low, low prices for the month,
Six-ninety-five for a Total Makeover, or,
With no money down, a Special Elevation of the Rear End.

And then, too soon, the news
Leaks in from the network, and it's time
To stack the napkins and clear the set.
It's been so nice
To visit with you this morning,
In this city where the weather slips
From one shade of gray to another,
As if we've always
Lived under a cloud of unknowing.
And may the rest of your day be
As bright as this beginning. And may
The good Lord guide your feet
Around whatever's steaming on the sidewalk,
And bring to your home
All those blessings you might have missed
While the oatmeal bubbled in forgotten pots—
The salary and the suburbs and the soup du jour.

Alligator Pears

Fat neck on a
potbelly bottom; hide green
and scabrous as a gator's snout;
flesh that could slide from
unripe to rotten in a day—
who knew them
by any other name? Back
in the South, in my boyhood,
it all made sense
with salt and lime and oil.
I scooped the socket out, crescents
of cream on a spoon, smooth
and chartreuse, the tongue
soothing itself on the taste. Who knew
where they came from, these Aztec idols
hung up on the sun, rough pouch
with a stone in its womb,
the must of a wet nut rising
like a bloated body from the swamp?
This pit fit my palm. I could,
like David, kill a man, then plant it
deep in his brow, a third eye
staring back at the brain, cold
compost of a corpse
that fed the roots and made
the pale leaves unfold. Who knew,
those dark years before we
felt the walls of our heart silt up
with slag and sinter, what tales
these leather bells would toll for us?

O Holy Night

Season of suicides and soup pots
Of the Salvation Army, tinsel
Tossed up to the tree's white star.

I walk through the canned carols
Of the mall, past the perfume counter
With its swollen air, a spray that barely

Holds back the odor of wet wool
And fumes rising from the armpits,
From the sacked gravel of the groin.

In one window, some Dada decorator
Has left his mannequin out naked
In the cold, fake frost on the fingertips,

Reindeer harness around the loins.
I know those cheekbones with their
Starved Eurasian highlights and that

Pre-Socratic smile on the blue lips.
She seems to be conducting
A chorus of noëls with a kitchen spoon,

Not minding the toy locomotive that
Chugs up her skull, or the boxing gloves
Where her breasts used to be.

Under the polestars of the parking lot,
A slow ribbon of red lights
Slides on the dark, and even the angels

Can't lift off, their halos frozen,
Ice on the wings. O holy night,
When every word I speak blows up in smoke.

Swampscape with Oil Platform

The cottonmouth slides out
Along the rot, fallen limb on a fallen log,
Its tongue a split lick that turns
The air dark around it, trembling
In the wake of the Evinrude.
Pole and bait shrimp, straw hat, whiskey
For a nip when nothing
But mosquitoes bite—we run the outboard
Down a sluggish basin by the mudbanks.

They say that fish lie low,
Secrets inside the shade, a cool stir
Under the sunken trusses of this
Oil platform abandoned in the swamp—
Rusted struts, deck at a deep angle,
Pump in a pitch of agony
Where it once sucked up the oozing crude.

We cast for cats and let our lines
Slant into the shadows, the pale bobs
Floating over lurk and flash.
However rich the waters, like gravy
Lapping at the boat, we didn't come
So much for what we might
Haul up on hooks, as for anything
The eyes could catch—wild swine around
The writhing roots of cypress,
Heron on their high spike heels,
And green sierras of the gator's back.

A thin slope of filaments
On the sleepy sheen
Measures how far we've gone, the sun
Pressing down on us

Until the day's packed tight into
This idle hour, as solid as solitude.
No coarse cry breaks the air; no splashes
Scar the smooth grain. However hard
The anchor holds, we drift
Into the long glaze and tilt of afternoon.

Living in OH

Small world, the newswise say: the mean and the main streets,
Hayseed and steel, three-piece families around the firebrick, all making
Crosscut numbers for the poll, a trial market for Frozen Fatfree Velveeta-
    on-a-Stick.

Where I live, in a split-level house near the heart of Highlow Hollow,
Just east of Euphoria, just west of the Fortunate Falls, midway
Through the moods and months of the year, in the slow days of
    Messidor,

Among the sons flailing their air guitars or jacking up jalopies, among
Daughters all named Jennifer or Heather, Dawn and Nicole, where the
    wives will
Spit on your best pants and press an iron to the fly, sizzling it flat,

I'm no Swinburne-Jones of the painted syllable, but a sub-contractor
Putting in the pipes and traps of the line, sweating the joints, my only
    hobby
Performing parlor tricks with blunt instruments and a marked deck.

Dead center in this settlement, on this square board of squares, where any
    of us
Could be kinged or kangarooed on the next move, we're testing out
The Second Law of Thermodynamics, Newton's notion that the world

Won't work without change, spontaneous response in a flow of heat:
Does entropy increase in this isolated system? Does the deep kiss
Chafe at the lips, or pass passion through the trading tongues?

We take all this with a grain of gestalt, like looking at
The duck-rabbit of Wittgenstein, its truth neither down nor fur,
But the eye suspended in liquid shifts, the shape of everything negotiable.

We've found that half-measures even out the odds, and have learned to speak
    speak
Not from the gutter or the dark study, riprap of books on a shaky case,
But from the mall, the Toyota showroom, making poetry safe for

The middle class, citizens of the sitcom and the barbecue, a tang of smoke
    smoke
Rising from the high-priced fat that drips and hisses on the coal, a cloud
That shadows the lawn a moment, then drifts far off into the ruins,

City of the blade and the broken bottle, city under siege by
Children of the gun, where bellies rumble like a subway braking in,
A scent of something to sink the teeth in, the tease of a greener ground,

As the weatherwoman smooths her locks on the late news, smiling
Through tornadoes, through floods that float the dead away, and then
    misreads her cue,
Tomorrow will be warm and human, another promise our kind can't keep.

Metairie Cemetery

Who walks among these graves?

No one. You make your rounds
On rented wheels, from a plot of in-laws
Stacked under the flat lawn
To the crowded vault of your old
Sicilian line, names of ancestors
Hammered out in wet stone.
Only the dead stay dry
This afternoon of faint rain.

What do you bring to these graves?

No Horatian platitudes, no bouquets
To smother the air. Every pilgrim
Carries himself on his own back.
Among the swampy parishes, past
Seasons of redbud and bird of paradise,
You bear the distant hints of north—
Cold sky, bleak leaves, the grass
Knuckling down in the dirt.

What do you seek among these graves?

Not the monuments to rebel bones
Or granite for the whores of Storyville—
Disasters and souvenirs. Here you breathe
The mossy origins, the dreams that
Worm their way inside your mind,
And winds from the tall memorial oaks
Like ghosts still sealed in your marrow,
Where the blood runs hard and sweet.

Drowning in Ohio

In the month of mildew, plunging thunderstorms
Crease the dark with their freak chandeliers,
Bully the roses and the loose roof.
A stink of rain
Rises from the asphalt, and the air
Bloats in a stupor of greasy swells, moping
Over the neighborhood.

Dog days with the mange . . .
Heat wraps itself around you like
A weasel on a Rhode Island Red, swelter
Even the attic fan can't suck up. The whole state
Lies down with a cool cloth on its forehead
Or moves its heavy feet in numb shoes,
Zombie with a drug habit.

Inside this downpour, the small town feels
Barbarous and raw.
You miss the spiky scent of grass, the insects'
Rhetoric by the evening porch, the moon
Looped in a cat's cradle of stars.
And the bay panes? It's like looking out a porthole
At a drenched horizon.

With any luck, a noonday sun will rout the clouds
And willows mop the mud away.
With any luck, the mercury will drop
Like a two-bit palooka, and the birds come back
To their vaudeville turns, slapstick
In the ruins of oak and pine. With any luck,
You'll find a rainbow purged of sullen promises.

Incompatibles in the Wild Light

Whether you're up to the ankles in
Snake Crick, or up to the neck
In Lake Lurleen, you can still feel

Fire ants in the wiregrass, hornets
Practicing in their paper hives
A million little stings from the South.

(And is this any worse than standing on
A crust of snow, under the frozen gutters,
Hypodermic of icicles with a sharp drip?)

Everything frightens you here, in the land of
Reptiles and child brides, catfish with their
Poisoned whiskers like Rumanian spies.

Somehow you've missed the blue heron
In the wetlands, purple plummet of wisteria,
Juleps newly minted under the Spanish moss.

Somehow you failed to hear the crickets
Rigging up their amps in the underbrush,
The moan of live oaks, the back porch guitars,

You cringing from a skink of fingers on
The juke joint keys, the gospel of pandemonium
Making the pulpits leap and sweat.

Even the lingo of pine tree and palm
Passes you by, your cold ears open only to
The pulpwood trucks, the twitter of politicians.

Have you come down here to civilize the fathers
And drag the freak children out of this
Salacious sun? Why don't you, instead,

Sit under the sweet olive and suck
A stick of sugar cane, and let the mockingbird
Recite our history like a syrup of sins?

Hawk on a fencepost; three dead rabbits in a ditch;
Copperheads asleep in the noonday dust. And all around,
The slippage of insects, raw ooze of heat.

And still you wait for a cool wind to
Twist the makeshift clouds, like flaws in a drawl,
And drain the shadows from this bloody ground.

Two

Looking for what was, where it used to be

WALLACE STEVENS

1945

In the war, you could choose between
Levels of evil, as if hell had its own dark ranks:
Mussolini made the trains run on time;
Hitler made the trains run over you on time.

But what do I know? I was born
The year the war ended, German by name, Sicilian by blood.
My father was 4-F with a busted eardrum;
My mother wore her hair up in a baker's loaf.

I had no uncles to bring me back a bayonet
Or a bad cough picked up in Paris from brandy and Gauloises.
The year I was born, there was kissing in the streets
And a crippled president dead in a pinetree cottage.

I've seen the pictures: Il Duce hanging by his heels;
The Fuehrer barking down his generals at the map table;
Ike in his tight jacket and the smile of a village simpleton.
I've seen the skulls stare out behind the wire fences.

No matter what Marx said, history does not repeat itself as farce—
It moves from tragedy to tragedy, and it has no end,
Only intermissions for the gin and the dancing girls,
For the axe that falls between the acts.

Cramped in my mother's womb, I might have been
A sailor on a U-boat, listening for the slow approach
Of the last torpedo, the waters trembling around me.
I might have been crouched in a foxhole, as rain rose to my neck.

Could I feel the Axis in my veins, the old Europe
That turned to mud under the boots and the heavy wheels?
What did I know about bodies and burned cathedrals?
I came out bawling, the only human thing to do.

Mardi Gras Indians

I'm no Spy Boy for the Wild Squatoolas,
But I've heard all the gods of Africa
Strike back in a saxophone, and I've seen
The black tribes fire out
From the shotgun houses of Valence Street,
That day before the ashes smeared
Dark and soft on our sins. They flare
In their savage satin like the brass beat
Of a tambourine, arms dripping old fringe
Ripped from a lampshade, sequins aflame
And rhinestones blinding the breast,
A plunge of plumes in a drop crown, and everything
Gaudy with gilt and glitter and glue.

O it's Mighty Kooti Fiyo, it's
Two-Way Pocky Way, when Big Chief Jolley
Swanks up in a cayenne suit. He's got
A Choctaw cheekbone and a Congo jaw.
He's got the good foot pumping like
The pedal on a boomboom drum. Somebody
Hand him a fatmouth beer and let
The voodoo loose, the second line kick in
Like a warclub on a skull marimba.

I'm no Flag Boy for the Wild Tchoupitoulas,
But I can feel the bloodrun of their strut
Free me to the streets, to the powwow
Spiked with feathers and a boozy whoop,
As the day bows down to their red bravado.

Grand Isle

Far south of the cat's-paw snowflakes
Furring the dusk in Ohio, deeper than
The black bogs and sloblands of Carolina,
We come to Grand Isle, sand and marshweed
Sliding against the Gulf whose warm waters,
Muscled upshore by a hurricane, can peel
An oak to its pith, can soak the horned hide
From a ten-foot gator. Even the mobile homes
Rise high on stilts, a waveway under
Each hoisted house where cypress nameplates
Swing in the wind: *Sans Souci, Coonass Heaven,*
Ed and Mabel's Last Retreat. Here the legends
Still brag down to us: how Amphyle Margot
Would parade his pet goose, amusing
The beachbrown children and the dowagers
Half-adoze on the hotel veranda, squawks
And argot in the salty air, where smugglers
Once slipped their creole loot to
The belles and proud fops who danced away
The graves of yellow fever; how Lafcadio Hearn,
Summering behind the breeze of mosquito screens,
Wrote his romance of the last island, remembering
That woman saved from the floods of 1893
By her wild hair tangled in a branch;
How tourists scrambled on the toy railway
That wheeled them to the sea and clacked back
To the vine-cooled cottages some businessman
Had gussied up from slave cabins
Set free for leisure and a season's profit.
Under brackish clouds that spoil the sun,
We turn, still white from winter, on the sand
Stinking with searoots and stranded crabs,
And watch the derricks stand offshore in haze,
A Stonehenge of steel struts, sucking out

The secrets of the deep. On the narrow road
Behind us, two rusted pickup trucks
Honk and pass, the far one dusting its way
To the bridge that brought us here,
A gray rainbow breaking from
The disconnected endless end of Louisiana.

Bedtime Legends near Esplanade

After the Barq's and the Big Red and the codfish cakes,
War whoops and a six-handed assault on the parlor piano,
After a run through every room of the house on North Broad,
Greased weasels where the inner child should be,

We slipped inside the loose pajamas, cousins from country and city,
And called for Mama C., great-aunt, widow with a limp,
To settle us like the soft sag of her old Sicilian face,
Ready for bed and the dreams she would wring our sleep with,

Not her monologue of *morphadites* on every corner in New York,
But a creole tale, her voodoo story with a dago twist:
In that tall house where the shadows lived, a lady of noble name
Locked her slaves on the upper floor, chained in the cruel light,

A woman who moved by day among the rich, the high families
Who sent their sons to France and taught their daughters the small arts,
Making the morning rounds, the afternoons of tea and politesse,
The silver service giving back the bent sheen of her face.

By night, should you linger near her grand mansion, idling
To bring the matchblaze to your slim cigar, or to breathe
The sweetened air of magnolias where the streetlamps burned,
You would hear the buried moans, the faint shaking of shackles,

A lash that cut deep across the black back of evening,
Louder than the whispers passed at noon behind the silken fans
Or the words swallowed as the wine went down in every glass,
Rumors that left their stench like the stone well in her yard.

And when she died, of poison or a bad heart or some spell
No one would claim, the crowd in midnight ribbons and bombazine
Broke the shutters open to the purifying sun, and found
The guttered rite of candles, the altar blessed with blood,

And one slow servant who would lead them to the top,
The long room like the hold of a trade ship, where living bones
Were ringed with iron links at wrist and ankle, their eyes
Starved deep into the head, dry tongues scraping the silence,

And just beyond the blind doors that faced the front, a balcony
From which she tossed the dead down into the wide maw of the well,
A stock of white spikes and skulls, rainwater soup so foul
The bottom seemed to heave and seethe with the odor of evil.

And lying stiff under the sheets, we thought we knew
The dark address of that house, three narrow levels rising far back
Behind a wrought railing, a fence with pickets like a pitchfork.
Sent off on errands of oysters or fresh bread from Esplanade,

We stopped across the street from those haunted stories and stared
Until we almost saw a glide of ghosts beyond the windows
And heard the air rankle with a clank and chant and screams,
Children who still believed the lies of early legends and late dreams.

Hurricane Lamp

When we fill the lamps, the waters rise,
And the families across from us
Stroke their pirogues through the deadend street.

How can the soot-slight glass of the chimney
Keep its flame against
A wind that beats both fists on every window?

Even if the flood damps down the fire ants,
There's still the sting
Of pine straw launched into night and skin,

Of cottonmouths that belly on the crest,
Writhing by
Like the lopped-off arms of black men.

Mama's busy at the stove, stirring up
A mess of neckbones,
Collards, dirty rice—but who could eat?

By the light that winces on the cracked wall,
Afraid of its own shadow,
I pull the pillow to my eyes and pray

For dry dawn out of darkness, for sunbows
Over the sucking drains,
For all the wicked and the wickless.

Trailers

Like the bowl of a tarnished spoon, the moon
scoops up the light and pours it over us,
the way you tip that bottleneck against
the rim of a Star Wars glass, Old Crow in the Coke,
flat taste turned sharp as an ice cube's clink.

So what if there's always some cocklebur
stuck on your socks, and a stink in the shower stall
like a week's worth of diapers? So what if you
waste whole days with your eyes one inch above
the flatfooted prose of a cop novel, wearing nothing
but huaraches and a sweatshirt, your breasts
legible under the name of some washed-out college?
Those games that others play in their suits and offices—
the peekaboo briefcase, the file drawers half-open,
scent of Obsession breezing back from the Rolodex—
won't work for you, not when your fingers make
a scrimmage in the M&Ms, or slip another Lucky
from the target pack, its logo gone up in smoke
at the scratch and crackle of a kitchen match.

We'll take the quiet here, out in the scrub
among the sweet corn and the cucumbers, no
neighbors raving like rain on a tin roof,
no clatter of trucks on a redball run. If we need
the novelty of noise, like a blue jay cocking its ear
from the crosspiece of a creosote pole, we'll
potshot the dump, the rats shifty in their whiskers,
dapper as Adolphe Menjou down on his luck.

In this lodestone for storms, this tornado haven,
where breakfast comes as cold bacon and biscuits
that defy the knife, where fossils of Juicy Fruit

ripen under the cocktail table, and oil slicks down
from a .38 placed on the armchair's upholstery,
we pay no mind to the philosophic seasons, winter
with its bone oblivion or May trees turning over
a new leaf. In this box of double-wide dreams,
we loll in the lowlands of desire, immune
to the slow injuries of time and rent and rings.

The Worst High School Marching Band in the South

We've seen you all before,
A spectacle of spectacles, thick
As the skull of a cheerleader in midleap—

The hornrimmed owls, the harlequins
Of brassy hair, the round
Astonished look of wired eyes.

Even at the homecoming game,
You never felt at home, not with
The bell curve of your horn

Turned up in the rain, so deep
No spit valve could shake it off,
Three spindly fingers and two left feet

Making of the muddy football field
Squeals and pleats between the lines,
A hidden message in the halftime mess.

Even then, you never knew the score.
In caps and epaulets, frogged out in braid,
Cuffs at highwater over loose shoes,

You brought up the sweaty rear
Of the Independence Day parade, always
A block behind the other bands, trailing

The waxed convertibles of the livestock queens
And politicians perched on the back seat
Like birds of prey, their cheap suits

Soggy in the noonday sun, their grins
Glinting like the gunsights of assassins,
Always at the tail end, following the firetruck

And the cop car, always missing the beat,
Snares and glockenspiels carried low as
Heavy shovels after the circus elephants.

The flag girls and the majorettes,
Tassels on their boots, batons and bunting
Stalled out like planes in a nose dive,

Shuffle and squint, a rictus fixed
In the face, as if they'd all tied for last
At the Scarlett O'Hara Look-a-Like pageant.

What big drums will wake you
To the life that lies impossibly beyond
The beehive hallways of high school?

What cymbals will go off
Inside your heads, like alarm clocks,
Spun metal ringing in the future's news?

For now, there's nothing you can do
But stagger in broken columns,
Like the ruined temple of forgotten youth,

Defiling the file, losing a step
With every bar, soused on Sousa,
Rapping out the cold cacophonies of pomp.

There's no law against bad music,
No tuba litigation, no policies forbidding
Saxophone harassment in the practice room,

Though we can hope, before you weave around
The wrong goal post in the wrong end zone,
That someone somewhere

Will put his foot down in time,
And two sudden flutes out of ten
Will sweeten the evening air.

Benjamin in the Salvage Yard

As we turned transparent with sweat
In the summer sun, he talked of
Pussy and half-pints and knives,
Those Saturday nights cut loose
From tire and steel, the slow wrestling
Of wrecks in my father's junkyard—
Benjamin, young enough to pass
As my older brother, black enough
No one would call us kin.

On drives to the dump, he taught me
Pedal and stick shift, making the clutch
Pop in the rickety pickup, cursing
My grind and jerk, more patient
Than that state instructor who,
Though he must have cooled his veins
With antifreeze, boiled over and failed me,
And said, because he could not
Flag down every driver on the road,
That boy's gonna kill somebody one day.

Benjamin, bony hero of the low life,
Virgil of the darker ways, I remember,
Months after you signed up your years
To the army, how you came back
In neat creases and olive cap,
And sat down at the family table
As if you had a place there, telling
Tales of the drill and the hard march
And orders to move out, my parents
Giving each other that fisheyed look,
Surprised by your poise before us
In the kitchen chair, and wondering who,
In the late fifties, in Louisiana,

Would be dumb enough to make this
Lanky chuckleheaded boy in a rank skin
Private, first class.

Problem Child

Scissors: I was never
Good at scissors. Paste was
My strong point, and glue, and the
Skinny clutch of clip and staple.

Even the priest with his mean
Mouth could not make my
Wayward hands go straight, like
Grandma at the Singer Sewer.

I liked the clean, uncluttered
Look of lines, dotted or drawn.
Why butcher them? Why shear
The smooth sheets to hash?

I would fuss over buttons, too,
And lace the wrong eyelets, as if
I'd been dressed by blind midgets
With a grudge against fashion.

And at the barbershop, I felt
Condemned to the chair, to the
Rake of blade and comb, stiff with
Visions of the bloody bandages.

The boys with cool and moxie
Knew how to peg a knife or
Lop the balls from a dead pig.
I came out of the cradle

With paws and primitive feet, body
Cramped against my own slow way,
Pinched and pathetic, rabbity amateur
Of the slingshot and the marble ring.

By the end of the day, I'd be so
Frazzled and beat down, you could
Spoon me out of my shoes—
Botch of the playground, apprentice oaf.

I took my comfort in
Tales of the glass slipper, the bridge
And the billy goat. And you could
Mute me with sardines and cheese.

And somehow I saw myself
In that legend of the crazy saint
Who turned to low amusements
At the Mass, to keep himself

From rising in a sudden trance
Above the candles: jokebook
Open by his gilded missal, and
A monkey chained to the altar steps.

Late Fifties on Front Street

Friday nights we'd swarm the downtown movie house,
Horror double-dosed with reels of rock'n'roll: *Them*, maybe,
And *The Girl Can't Help It:* a gang of edgy ants
Souped up on nuclear mutation, barbell biceps
On the bugs, and eight thighs strong enough to crush
A dozen patriotic dumb platoons; but no irradiated queen
Could make us blanch and sweat more than the
Breasts of Jayne Mansfield, paps our papal science
Confirmed as lungs, external lungs, bellows too big
To breathe inside her body, and barely held back
By the blouse that aimed and launched them towards us,
Nothing stranger in this universe to Catholic boys, not even
The mile-high marcelled hair of Little Richard
And the keyboard booms that shook the common decencies
Of Mom and God and Ike and Sister Mary Ethelred,
All our organs juiced and fried, ground zero
For that detonating scream. The grade school girls
Who scared us with their extra inches, their perfumed poise,
And whom we sat behind to tease in the silvered dark,
Were more remote than any monsters on the screen,
Though less alarming than those knockmedowns
That Hollywood hung over us, that we could feel each time
The ear-piercing pitch of a black man in baggy pants
Broke the sound barrier, a shrill of syllables
Outpacing every hormone bent on hell, an eerie freedom
Echoed in the balcony, that segregated tier
Of popcorn catapulting down like angry manna, asterisks
To any pleasure heaven might allow, the whole house
Leaping and screeching in the weekend jitters of release,
Until the flashlights stunned the aisles and ushered us
Out to the southern night where mothers waited at the curb,
Cars idling in the scorched cloud of their exhaust.

2 *Drink Minimum*

Not often, and only when
a double sawbuck rubbed
its Jackson against your jeans,
would you go straight
from the late shift to Bourbon,
lightbulbs racy around
the Creole or the Tiger's Den
or the Gay Paree, where barkers
flashed the front door
on a sigh of thighs, a split-
second chance at flesh.
Back in the dark tier
where you sat, the B-girls buzzed
from tips to table, rows
away from the raised stage,
its blue spot fixed on
flanks like pink siding,
Maypole for a partner in the hump
and sway. You chose a club
too cheap for union scale,
for those old farts blowing up
a storm of stale airs;
Top 40 45s
came crackling through the kinks
of the low-tech speakers—
a sass of saxophones
smeared on the jailbait beat,
or teen crooners pouring out their
loneliness through the nose. At the limit
of your own slim means,
and the toll of entry so high,
why suck on Jax or Dixie,
both bottles gone warm
at once, swaddled in sweat,

before the first even
cleared your throat? You took
two shots of Scotch, rocks
and a thumb of hard water,
pale and slippery as a bar
of old soap on the tongue.
Though rumors claimed these women,
Sextana and Belle Bottom
and Cherie la Femme, were all
dykes in spiked heels
and flame-retardant hair,
who could watch them tease off
layer after layer, a kind of
onion arousal meant to
resurrect the dead center
of your dreams, and see nothing but
a slow death in drag?
In that spin of fringe from pasties
taped to the nipple, and the hips
strung down to a thin
glitter like ice, and the grind
of sharp shoes bracing
a body that could put your eyes out,
you got the point. Well after
the stroke of midnight and the last
stutter of drums, the drinks
no more than memories in your marrow,
you rose through smoke, through the sour
slipstreams of heat, and found
the streets now gleaming in a wet
hiss of wheels, and heard behind you
the catcalls rising, the dance
still fanned by applause, steamed up
like a rancor of sudden rain.

Evening Services on North Rampart Street

You can waste your days and grace at the Easy Action
Or the Second Line Lounge, or chain yourself to the 8 ball
Snug in the pockets of the Auction Block (Ladies Invited and Respected),
Saving your soul on the layaway plan, no penance down,
Eternity to pay, and a last deal cut over the coffin,

Or you can come humbly to that church like a Legion Lodge,
Paint peeling from the slats and the stair rail, a homemade sign
Nailed up for the services: the Rev. Wyletta L. Pomroy presiding
At the Prince of Peace and Israel Baptized in the Southern Light.

They're testifying in their white robes and miters, the bishops and the
    brethren
And big women like angels with a thyroid problem, playing out
A cross-rhythm of the gospels on upright and drums, in one hand
The torch of a tambourine, and in the other, Jesus on a stick.

The Rev. Wyletta L. Pomroy calls up two legends from the dead:
That half-black, half-Mohawk singer from the Windy City,
Miss Leaf Anderson, who set this house in order, backed up
By her chorus of spirit guides, Queen Esther and Father Jones;
And Mother Catherine Seals, who always entered her Temple of Innocent
    Blood
Preaching feet-first from a hole in the roof, her mission there
To raise all the bastard babies of the neighborhood.

And before you feast at the laden tables, the long boards cramped
With a voodoo sampling of saints and candles, turkeys and cakes,
A star-spangled flag draped over the headdress of a hardwood chief,
Put yourself in the Reverend's thick, prophetic hands, as the children do,
Dunked like doughnuts in a liquid grave, then spun dry in a spasm,
A trance with the gowns belled out, eyes burning from the body's dark.

Edified at the altar, sanctified in the tank, tongue taking on
The voice of John the Revelator, the grunts of Sitting Bull,
You'll turn from bad liquor to the Lord, and feel that spark
As if you'd touched a live wire let down from heaven:
A soul in shock: ghost on a pinwheel in the voltage dance.

To John, in Alaska

I know by heart where the South is, and I've learned
For more than thirty years what the Midwest means,
But where in hell is Alaska? If I had any sense
Of sure direction, could tell up from down, left from right,
I'd put my blind finger on the map and find you,
Dear friend living somewhere, as I hope, near the white
And godforsaken wastes of Canada, for it has long been
My wild ambition to say one day in a poem the sacred names
Of Saskatchewan and Saskatoon, that slippery spill of syllables.
So, am I close? Or have you once more passed beyond
The reaches of my mind into the distant mists of geography,
Another third grade lesson I slept through after lunch?

I know you've grown up now to middle age, and may be rich,
For even in that discontiguous state a doctor must pull in
More than enough money from trappers with a clumsy touch
Or oilmen seeking some moose for a meaningful relationship.
But I remember the holy days when we met, both of us
On our knees in the minor seminary, either at prayer
Or sentenced to penance in the dining hall for some fool prank,
You a stranger from the federal sands of Florida, a beach city
Where rockets left their wakes of flame across the skyline,
Me a native of the bayous and the rainy streets, a junkman's boy
Sweating through the acetylene summers of Louisiana.
We shared the dark music of our humor, sly souls among the monks.

Fast friend, you lasted longer than I did, a legend
On the ball fields and in the memories of eccentric men.
Do you still bow your head in the Sunday pew, solemn
And smiling and good, tall father of a lanky family?
I've put behind me that candied heaven, that jujubilee,
All those promises that come melting from the tongue,
And placed my faith in sonnets and sonatas, and in
The nervous fallen arms of love. Is there really an Alaska,

Somewhere past the continental edge? I've got my bearings now,
And still your face recedes into that question I hate to ask—
Not where you've gone, but what have we come to,
So many shaken years away from our lost communion.

Three

It is hard to be a prig in New Orleans. The courtesy and grace of a people so convivial and so erotic make the sterner kind of Puritanism difficult, and it comes to seem ungentlemanly, boorish, to insist upon moral issues of a political or social character.

EDMUND WILSON

Storyville

You can make it illegal, but you can't make it unpopular.
—Martin Behrman, mayor of New Orleans

I

In the whore album, the cracked plates
pieced back from the desk of Bellocq,
that waterhead, that frog-eyed dwarf,
he would let the light expose
the postures of appetite, the patient negatives
of flesh. Eyes forward or astray, hair wound up,
breasts familiar as faces, they felt
their bodies staring at the lens, a few stripped free,
a few cinched in Sunday swank, roses at half-mast,
hats abrim with dead feathers—and some heads
wrapped in a bandit mask or scraped down to black.

2

Wining boy in a boxback coat, foulard
and a loop of chain, he could sport the women
with a rooster strut, let the cuffs
shoot out and the pegtops slide easy
on his high buff shoes, fives shades darker
than his face—that's Mister Jelly Lord,
the creole snoot, godchild of the good voodoo,
Miss Eulalie, who pinned him to the name
he slipped out from, Ferdinand, fading like the voices
she called up from a water glass, spook stuff
the whores paid heavy gold to hear.

3

Miss Moment, the piano fake, hamhock of a woman,
first put his fingers on the keys,
but he took the blues from Mamie Desdoumes,
as all day she moaned and testified
I stood on the corner, my feet was dripping wet,
her right hand minus a double knuckle,
knees pumping time, her hard voice scratching
at the four borders of Storyville,
Basin by North Robertson, St. Louis by Customhouse,
where his hot rambles rang the chandeliers, lit
by bordello tips and a smile for notoriety.

4

Any buck with an itch and a two-dollar bill
could mate them in the *Blue Book,* that misspelled map
to the whore mansions, the camelback *maisons de joie,*
guide to a good time in bad prose, the scarlet women
branded by legends of White or Colored, Octoroon or Jew.
Passed out at depot and saloon, its pages,
around the poisoned remedies for clap, promised everything
from ragtime to damsels, from Sappho on the sofa
to the Only Female Cornetist in the Tenderloin.
And all this—the nude danseuse, the darky orchestra—
to skin the trick's sad need for a minute's warmth.

5

Dark drape over his skull, as if he'd taken
the veil and final vows, he bent
behind the camera, a Bantam on three legs,
waiting for the courtyard dogs to sniff
some distant brick beyond the frame,
for the half-dressed ladies to leave off

blinking at the sun, at the slow day
balled up in back of him, always waiting
for the moment to compose itself
and the shutter, in his calm hand, to open
all their agile secrets to the glass.

6

Wonders and abrasions! Loose hair flung to the sun
over a balcony rail, castwork of lyre and fleur-de-lis,
or dandled down the end of a garden bench.
Starched maids in the parlor; grits and grillade
hot on a scrapbook afternoon. And some drummer
with cases of sweet water, garters, and lace,
softsoaping the whores for the towel concession.
In a boudoir, they're staging the jezebel special,
stogies stuck in their middle lips, as the Suicide Queen,
forty times a failure, tries again—crossplanks on the track,
axe nagging her neckbone, X inked on a scrawny heart.

7

Ringmistress of the circus stunts, blunt
as the bayou cypress she was born by,
French Emma learned to raise a jaded lap
while Jelly Roll, eyes high behind the screen
he'd slit a view through, primed his piano:
Ladies and gentlemen, we are now in the jungles.
Everyone of you are animules. Bring on the dyke duet;
and Miss Olivia, wet from the oyster dance;
and that bareback woman lifting her hips
to the pony's stones and pizzle, the same horse
her unmossed daughter rode hard all afternoon.

8

Corruption, too, of the tongue:
as when the jazz joint of George Foucault,
that barkeep whose name the whiskey-lappers
slurred to a stew, was slicked back
to a native tease of syllables,
the Fewclothes Cabaret; or when at midnight,
inside the Unexpected Saloon and Rifle Club,
the clarinet king would blow, his big feet
braced against the bandstand lest his breath
hurl him backward with a shotgun kick,
the low runs roaring like a hurricane from hell.

9

Lacklove madonna of the honeyed cunt,
this one turns her blonde body   ·
for Papa Bellocq, all slope and shadow
to his unalarming look, sweet slant
pillowed on the wicker lounge; and this one,
a puzzle of broken flesh bound back
at the haunch, a gap like a garter belt,
stands in black stockings, ripped neck
and no head, arm disjointed, healed only
by the patch between her thighs
and the spackled spread of her breasts.

10

When Tony Jackson, the gal boy, vamped in
at the Pig Ankle, the Big 25, the Nanoon Saloon,
all the ivory poachers took notes. He could
pole down the bottom, flute through the high end,
arias to coon tunes, his squat lips making
the panther growl or icing the filigrees.

Even Jelly Roll, warmed up on himself all night
while the whores lolled back to his blues,
felt his bones melt from derby to pearl spats
when the professor, pomade in place, diamonds crackling,
spun the whole room around his black axis.

II

In the District, the madams sipped,
at their monthly meetings, a plush champagne,
queens pissing the profit away, swish of silk
and furs sweating at the neck, a parlor parody
of good women doing good for god's sake,
Society of Venus and Bacchus doling their peters' pence;
while in the Rampart cribs, beer bucket
under the bed by the chamberpot,
the black half-dollar whores pulled up
their shifts, always open where the jambs
abut the stud traffic on the banquettes.

12

Wanting a curse or a cure, believing in
the dogma of a black cat's bone, they sent for
Miss Julia, cross-eyed woman of the backward walk,
whose gris-gris could close a rival's cunt
or bring down the gleet with goat nuts, the pox
with blood from a wasp. What relics had the sway
of Follow-Me Water or Bend-Over Oil? What novenas
on St. John's Eve could draw a lover back
like the sand of lodestones, or make him stay
with the touch of a pronged root, the bedsheets
smooth as goofer dust from a hoodoo's grave?

13

Outside the hoodwink of his camera, he had
no friends, spoke of one whore only, Adele,
her name not tagged among the brothel faces.
Was this her kiss-curl spilled down the brow?
Did she lean toward him, breasts brimming
from her Mother Hubbard, that one-stop dress;
or toast the sporting life in her striped stockings,
tilt of an elbow on the table, near to
the rye bottle and the noonday clock? With a duckstep,
a voice pitched up like a creole squirrel, he lived
deep inside the helpless instincts of his eye.

14

When the women screamed, their time come
to push and twist and bleed, they summoned up
the spry hands of Dago Annie, who lugged
her satchel by a sprung strap and held their heads
until the tremors quaked away, calling for quick light,
clean rags, for water boiled in a basin,
jacking their legs back and reaching in,
a cool touch, soft and strong, trained to
unscrew the baby from the womb—
trick babies swaddled in the attic, sudden sons
and daughters of the daughters of the dark.

15

Goodbye to Miss Thing and Stingaree: the uptown johns
can't break the *Hesitation Blues*, now that the Navy
shut the District down. Goodbye to Eight Ball,
Bang Zang, and Titanic, and the hall of mirrors
crossbreeding the naked dance: now it's
bootleg bodies in the Tango Belt, dark doorways

where they swab the sailor's deck. Goodbye to Birdleg Nora
and Knock on the Wall: all the cornfed hookers,
gasbags, and drowsy octoroons, unhoused
from the touts and the stickpin millionaires,
have passed the last assignments of the evening.

Four

—Home is where the dead are—

RANDALL JARRELL

Time Zones

Five years shy of the century's end,
And a fin away from the last
Of two fishtail millenia, I've reached
The midway mark, half a hundred years,
Beads of the abacus strung out like
Bald heads knocked against each other,
Coldcocked in the summing-up.

Half a life in Ohio, a half-life
Counted by decay—and before that,
The boot-sucking snows of Michigan, a beach
In California where the brain went dry,
And down the dog-eared sepia, the faces
Slipping as a new soul drips
From the bloody womb of the South.

Now, in late summer, the sun
Works its way through the time zones,
Low and fat, and a slow cloud
Ghosts over me, crossing my hand
With its darker self. Where the two
Touch at the end of the line,
I write through my own shadow.

Shucking

My father lets down
The little drawbridge of his pickup truck,
A span of plywood planks on the back gate
Held level by hook and chain,
And dumps from the damp burlap
A load of locked doors
We've bought to break and enter,
Taking our spade-shaped knives
To the sharp and silted ridges of the oyster shells.

Almost safe inside the heavy canvas gloves,
Mule-brand, the fingers chewed through
By snags of ragged metal his acetylene
Cut back from the junked bodies of cars,
We look for leeways in the trap,
Any edge the blade can pry and widen,
Leverage to spring the hinge. I set aside
The hard ones for my father's savvy hands.
From the lusters of the bottom lid,
We split the raw attachments
And pour it all in a plastic pail—
Brine and gill plates and mantle—
My mother's turn now to turn
This plump meat seasoned by the sea
Into soups and stews and po-boy loaves
(Dredged in cornmeal, drowned in deep fat).

It's one more long Sunday when dinner waits
For my brother to drive down, late,
Through the pinesap airs of Hammond,
And for my sister to bring herself, late,
Across the white bridges, twin humps
On the billowed back of Lake Pontchartrain.

And so my father and I stand opening
The closed chambers, the cold valves,
And from these cups of calcium
Drink to each other a liquid
Of salt and grit, the oysters
Easing down like lumps in the throat.

Family Possessions

It is the mother they possess,
    Who gives transparence to their present peace.
    —Wallace Stevens

Rotten grapefruit on the ovary, roadblock in the bowels,
The liver suddenly a lie, rogue cells
Raiding the pink frontier of the lungs—
Cancer, thy name is lesion.

Sucking the dry breath of forgetfulness, open to
The lullabies of steel under the green sheets,
She slept through the probe that peeled away
The secret leeches, sponge lapping at the crosscut stitch.

Nurse-news in the waiting room; tears and relief:
Half the sick attachments knifed out, and half
Still buried in the deeper reaches, and what's left
Sampled for the cold prophecy of slides.

Pain promised; flashbacks of pain; pain its own sun and shadow.
All those guilty checks we sent, laying in a lifetime
Supply of trash bags from the crippled vets,
Perpetual lightbulbs from the blind, all those dollars that bought

A circus for burnt children, labs for the leaky heart,
Now deliver their dark dividend, like prayers
Whose answers fan out in multiple choice,
Not one right item in the patchwork lines.

We remember the night before, and the awkward priest
Balanced by platitudes, placing on her tongue
The deathtrip victuals of viaticum, and on her brow
Oils to ease a passage into the next expectant life;

And how the odor of one lily, insidiously sweet,
Big white earhorn for a deaf god, filled the room
With a smell of piety that bullies and bedevils,
Like the putrefying stump of an angel's wing;

And how the nuns, slacked in fashions five years behind,
Cheered up the overcast with their breezy chat; and how
Midnight swelled with premonitions, whispers too tired
To rise above the level of the stricken wish.

Now, rigged up to clear solutions that drip
From a Bauhaus coatrack, eyelids lashed to the cheek
As if sutured shut, she pries herself back from
A world so blue and slow it seems the sum of unspent summers,

And not this rain-begotten, rain-erasing spring
That teaches us the alphabet of the ill:
IC and IV and the robot purr of the CAT scan.
Stalled over Cokes and banned tobacco by the parking lot,

We talk ourselves around the random family years:
Dreamsicles from the ice-cream bike; cayoodle suicide,
A six-foot chain launched over a five-foot fence;
Catholic kisses steaming up the sockhop chaperones.

So much for the past; so little for the future.
The last azaleas give off a glow like radiation, a wet
Half-life of petals going down for the count,
As in her veins the blood plates pale and disappear.

Circling the bed cranked to an angle of repose,
We stare past the Jell-O and statistics, sibling
Seers of the 4th Sign, reading between the charts,
The frets and forces we're all dying to deny:

Shunt in the chest, that open wound in which
Skilled hands will pour the toxic drench of chemistry;
Turbans and permanent waves warming up
A skull bald as a Dachau Jew; fevers rising

Like a hunter's moon, and fear in a swab of sheets;
Bucket for the queasy heaves, brought on by
Mopwater and the afterlurch of lunch; the lagging
Plasmagoric siphon of life from a plastic bag.

Day by danger, safe by degree, she inches out
Across the barrens of the body, ghostland whose end
Remains a promise of remains, like X-rays gazing
At the bone-bottom, beyond the interrupted eye.

And over the long wire, states away, where everything we love
Comes back an echo from the brink, we'll listen for
Her quick of breath or silent slippage in the line,
The ring of broken circuits closed at home.

Pilgrimage

the music of decay was the music of redemption
—Osip Mandelstam

Bootheels on the bottom rung, butt
Stuck on the barstool, and three beers
Past toting up these longneck empties—
Subtraction being my only numerate gift—
I'm talking to Fred of Fred's Lounge,
In Mamou, Louisiana, the two of us
Alone in the air-conditioned dark of afternoon:
That last sick fish in the bibs and gimme cap,
Red Man softening his jaw, has floundered
Back to the evils of the workday sun,
His coin still spinning, calling up
The frenzied French of some jukebox two-step
I couldn't hope to construe, even if both eyes
Were drained and level and locked in on
The same jars of pig's feet and pickled egg.

I've angled down six states to hear
Fred unravel these yarns, legends of market Saturdays
When Revon Reed, microphone in the back booth
Rising from a mausoleum of dead Dixies, would open up
The Cajun caterwaul on KUEN, bare morning
And already the dance floor woozy with
A wash of alcohol, the waltz and the pigeonwing.
From the coulees and the cattle ranch, or the green
Spikes of rice in the floodfields, from the prairies
Of cotton and the flats of sugar cane, they come
In their weekend dresses and pressed pants—
Even that breadman stalled on his rounds, handing out
Warm samples of Evangeline Maid; and those teachers
Hired here from the motherland, their mission to

Purify the wayward tongue of Acadia; and the teenage atheist
Who dogs the daughters of the town cop and the chiropractor.

Fred sweats another brew across the grain, down payment
On the ticket I've reserved to Oblivion,
Window seat in the smoking car, ears still eager
As he whines away with his bayou haiku, his gumbo strut,
All the spice and license of the lowlands.
I've made this pilgrimage to leave my prints
On the pink beerocracy of cinderblock, to beard the ghosts
Of Arceneau and Fontenot and Thibodeaux,
Fiddles sizzling in a fat squall of accordion,
'Tit fer and guitars tingling through the tunes
Like skeeter drills in a trapline swamp, and on the roof
That tall antenna siphoning off to heaven
A case of this lubricated music, where the angels
Kick back on a cloud, their halos raked low,
Their lyres too lazy to keep up with
The syncopated spoons and the nubbly washboards,
As the band bears down on *Colinda* or covers
That mournful classic, *Hold My False Teeth*, making
Every molar this side of the Mississippi ache with gold.

There's no brassy hair at this quadrille;
In this stretch of the woods, no nymphettes in tube or tanktop
Abrade the air with their bounceables; here,
No one guzzles from grief or self-defense. I've done
The Opelousas jitterbug at Slim's Y Kiki; I've been
To Boo-Boo's for the crawfish race, and killed
A Ville Platte moonjar at Snook's; but this room,
Sleepy as the single stoplight on Main Street,
Wakes in me an echo of its quickstep days,
Till I can almost hear that singer's catchweed call
And the froggy gargle of his r's, and someone shouting
Don't drop the tater as the tune swings in.
You can still, in loose translation, pass a good time
At Fred's Lounge, in Mamou, Louisiana,

If Fred unwinds his tangled tales
And hoists another bottle to the bar, this one
On the house, his house, too many miles below
The one I've travelled from, a frozen outpost
In a foreign tribe, no chinaberry bush
Or bloody petals of Confederate rose, no spirits
Lifted to the shrine of pixilated grit.

Louisiana Elegies

in memory of Seraphia Leyda and Raeburn Miller

Now, at the blackboard, you could write
With your own bony finger, chalk talk
On an agate afternoon, parsing the poems,
Setting the questions for the last row
To stumble through, their pencils worn down
At both ends, reason and revelation
More remote than the deadline's edge.

Here, my lesson still unlearned, it's the month
Of slip and attrition, bulbs pressed far
Into the earth like dry hearts, waiting
For April and the sun's release, for May
When willows flinch in the spiked wind.

From the backward bayous of Eunice, from the oil
And bluebonnet legacies of Austin,
You brought your warm wits, your minds
Not tempted by the empty resonance
Of the classroom and the self-applauding page,
Your voices still patient in my ear, easing
The hard passages, the steep degrees.

For Seraphia, that ritual at the altar rail,
Vows taking root in the womb, before the rings
Cracked and the quirks of children taught her
How much the heart will scar before it heals.
And for Raeburn, the whisperings of same to same,
Love breeding secrets on the caught breath,
In the plague of deep attachments.

For one, the deep shade of invasion, betrayal
Of bad cells in the breast, before

A year of rays and the radical knife.
For another, the blood drummed down to spondees,
The stress leveled on machines that read
A sudden null scansion of the line.

Clippings lay out your lives, black data
Stiff in their boxes, above which your faces
Pose again in the grain of photographs,
Stubbles of light that hold you to
The pulped aftermath of pine, paper so thin
It tears in half at my smudged touch.

Whatever heaven you belong to, the gospel's
Golden elevations or a paradise of worms,
You stand here, now, at my shoulder,
On the stone side of the real, witness to
The day's speed and the night's treason.
And though you make no ghostly claims on me,
I take up the errands of the dead.

Listening to My Mother Breathe

Afraid she'll suffer in her sleep, and my father,
Deaf with a pierced eardrum and his years,
Will snore on, dead to the world,

We rig the cheap remote in an open window,
Plastic half of the set my sister bought
To overhear her baby in a distant room,

Almost a toy, wirefree, one step up from
Two tin cans linked on a string.
Red receiver head-level near my bed,

All night I stay up with
The heavy wave-like cresting of her breath,
A tide that evens out its pulse and lull.

Was it this way in the womb? Did I feel
The waters lap and fall, the birl
Of blood making its steady round?

The air sighs in and out, a dark release
Amplified against my ear, an easy
Heave and halt and letting go.

Sometimes she murmurs in her dream,
An undertow of speech too deep
To clear the mind, brought on by

Millions of sick cells or the pills that
Give her visions in the day's distress:
As she saw, once, in the dim corner

Of an afternoon, a child pleading, screaming,
Cries and fears she could not cure,
Heart helpless in the false light.

No matter how much
I shift and sweat, lean closer to
The static of broken syllables, they speak

Nothing to me, no more than
A shred of words, foreign
Soundings from the mother tongue.

Now, white swaddling the pink skull, her hair
Shuffles on the pillowslip, lank hanks
Razored by the frays of chemistry.

And then the pace comes calm again,
A soft surge, drowse of the metronome,
As if she lay under a spell,

Waiting, as I do, for the warm wake
Of a voice, a slip of breath
That will rise as long as I listen.

Oscillating Fan

1

Heat rises; cold comes down.

And yet we feel that hell
Is beneath us, and heaven somewhere
Above the high ice-crystal of the clouds.

2

Heat rises; cold comes down;
Humidity

Sticks in the middle
Where we live,

Air wrapped around us
Like the black shawl of Sicilian widows,

Or fingers on the windpipe,
The finishing touch.

3

Heat rises; cold comes down.

Hanging halfway up the wall,
A fan sings out
Like Sinatra in that movie scene,

"Summer Wind" in the Village,

When the world was still
Streetball all afternoon, before
The boys turned into

The menace of men, cool
And smooth as cheap suits.

4

Heat rises; cold comes down.

With a hitch, a palsy in the pulse,
The blades
Snick in a sour circle,
Bringing to a head
The dead breath of the day.

5

Heat rises; cold comes down.

Wheel in a wheel in a warm room,
The fan would
Scan the wet flesh,
Skin on skin, and stir
The white ring from a cigarette,
Pushing the smoke to a neutral corner.

6

Heat rises, cold comes down,
But the fan can't
Make up its mind, any minute now

Reversing itself to no end
In a slow refusal of the absolute.
Whatever moves us

From east to west in an even sweep
Comes back again—
Groan of the ellipse, stalled orbit of the earth,

Eternal return always on the level,
But never north, and
Not south, not south, not south.

Elegy for Clifton Chenier

> Sometimes it just be that way.
> —Buckwheat Zydeco, in concert

Big Hohner hotwired to the amps, he could
Kick back the darkness,
Pushme-pullyou of the blues, his brother
Thumbing down the steel ribs
Of a washboard, making the music dirty.

Gold gleam where the knuckles bend and the duct tape
Silvers half a handstrap, sweatshine
In the rampageous pitch of his curls,
A three-piece suit irradiant
As an oilpatch rainbow on a rutpool—

O zydeco, the beans ain't salty, the squeezebox
Don't miss a lick from
Pig squeal to purr to alligator growl;
From Mamou to Opelousas,
It's *Hot Tamale Baby* with the *Highway Blues,*

Ma Negresse in a two-step with *Jolie Blonde,*
Fiddles outfoxed by the saxophones,
Frottoir rubbing out the triangle's chime,
All boneslip and buttslap, fastfingered
Chanky-chank of his Red Hot Louisiana Band.

Now there's no breath left in the pleats,
Collapse of the last accordion: no more
Tous les Temps en Temps at the Bamboo Club,
No more *Parti de Paris* honking down
The dance floor of the Blue Goose Lounge.

We're holding a *fais-dodo* he'll never play
Or wake from. But even here,
Where snow sticks in the dark hollows
And weeds glint in the wind,
We can hear him laugh: *Mais oui, cher.*

Where I come from, the crawfish got soul.
And we can feel the swamp steam
Rising out of the tape reels, no bayou gloom
But the ghost of a black man,
Downhome ruckus pumped out from an upbeat heart.

On My Mother's Death

In member of our dear belovely Mother
—inscription on a headboard at Holt Cemetery, New Orleans

In the end, she wanted the end,
The one-way dark with no exit,
A door that would hush and close
On the hard clamor of this world.

From this end, she could hear her end,
That far call and welcome,
That bare blank beyond which
Heaven settles all its promises.

And taking heart, before her heart
Paused, and her breath came
Light as a spring wind
Smoothing down the down on a dove's breast,

She looked up, and let the light inside her
Part the darkness like a miner's lamp,
The long rays reaching
To the end of the end she wanted.

Pelican Tracks in the Rain Dreaming

after a painting by Johnny Warrangula Tjupurulla

This panel of stringbark straightened over a fire,
Its hatchings traced by the stem of an orchid, or by
Bristles of human hair dipped in the reds of revelation,
In ochre pounded from a stone, in aboriginal black—
Why should this painted pattern, born of a stranger South,
Mean so much to me? From the outback of bone poles
And the bandicoot, witchetty grubs and goannas,
Its lines bring round the vision I now take title to:

Half-earth, half-water, and the webfoot at home
Wherever it moves, printing itself on the mud shore,
On a world drained by the low tides of appetite
And washed by tears seeking their own level, a saltway
Drawn down from densities of darkness in an open eye—
Everything sinking, everything rising again in the mind.

Black Baptist Funeral

in memory of Lelia Green

We've come early, in late morning,
To Doyle's Funeral Home on Fourth Street in Slidell,
No preacher yet behind the chapel podium,
No hands trembling over the piano keys, only a box
Flanked with flowers, the lid open, and her face
Still freckled under the undertaker's dust,
A sleepy smile played out in the calm of the casket.

Soon the bare pews buzz with babies, small boys
In the aisles, restless as the dresses of women
Bright with big blooms, and big hats
Crisp and beribboned, in cool colors,
Straw brims slanting down the brow, more like
A cakewalk than a Wake and Dismissal.
The programs, laid out with their order of events
And verses and supporting cast, we all use
To push the air around, the air that hangs
From the heavy Processional of family loss
To the Viewing of Remains when her service ends.

Blood runnin' home in the veins,
The reverend says, in a rustle of linen and amens,
And now Sister Green been called home.

And it's a long way from Amite, Louisiana,
To death, a trail winding through the pine woods
And the cottonmouth waters of the swamp,
Through two days a week of sweeping and mopping,
One eye on the steam iron, the other on the soaps,
Wisp of a cigarette drifting over
The aroma of red beans seasoning on the stove,
Salt meat and sausage, a hot loaf of po-boy bread,

And Lelia laughing at all our jokes, her lips
Held tight around the secrets we tell her, those petty sins
We've learned to keep back from our parents . . .

And after the prayers and eulogies, a solo hymn
I've never heard before, having been raised
On Latin sacraments and the chanting of monks,
Though I know the holy waxwork of Professor Longhair,
His left hand the mallet of the Caribes, his right
A tipsy tightrope over an alley of broken bottles,
Every note falling somewhere between
The fishfries of Friday night and the funerals of Monday morning.

Out under the sun, we're with her in our Dodge Spirit
That tails the slow cortege, a shining line of
Cousins and nephews, aunts and a lone daughter,
The Cleveland sisters she rode a dog night and day to see,
Squeezed in a narrow bus seat; and for once
The cops hold back the world to let her pass—
Red lights mean nothing to the dead.

When my mother died, in a spring already past
The last blush of azaleas, the wind blowing
Through shanks of cemetery grass cut down
Within an inch of their lives, we brought Lelia up
To sit beside us in the shade of the canopy, hers
The one black face among the mourners there,
For the blessing and the mute baffles of goodbye.

Just off the Dixie Ranch Road, where her house
Stood framed forty years under the oaks, we turn
Down a dirt track so cramped the cars must park
Halfway in the ditch, wet ruts of a lane
Winding deep in the country where no one goes
Except to dump their trash or bury the dead
In the homemade graveyard of the Greens,
The mud scooped out with a backhoe, and everyone

Swabbing the sweat of early August, waiting
On those pallbearers built like linemen for the Saints,
Suits bunched up over muscle, dark stains under the arms
As they slide her body from the hearse, the crowd
Closing in to hear the preacher's brief about
What lies here, and what lies ahead, and what lies . . .

Words of heaven float over the broken stones,
The crosses leaning in the weeds, and mean
No more than a promise of clouds that might
Bring a moment's peace to this raw plot, before
The long parade of the living steps back
From the grief and the heat and the hollow ground.

Endsheet

Does the world need one more poem
About Ohio, or the heavy
Sexual incense of the South,
Or dead mothers rising in the dusk?
I could give you lines
Lifted from the drift of history, or plucked
In sudden rapture from the air:
Sumerian wheels and the ziggurat; the sky
Clearing its throat of thunder, another flashback
In the story of the storm. I could
Take you out of here, out of your self,
To the pink and green Bermudas, Berlin of cloudy stone,
Or back to the barefoot Etruscans climbing up
The wine-vine hills of Tuscany, far beyond
These acid colors idling over the franchise strip—
Burgers in neon, long tubes buzzing above
Complimentary coffee in the muffler shops—
A *paradiso* of the waste places
Some still prefer
To the blue of Hockney pools, believing
Pleasure has no principle but the real.
For every one who lives
Along the mudsucked Nile, or by
The black alleluvias of the Mississippi, or in
The lassitudes of moonlight
Lapping the seawrack sand, there's one
Who hears the faucet eking out
Each drop down to the dishwater, a penance
Of moments spent and left behind. If you want
The buckwheat honesties, the burlap truth,
Essence of vanilla in a mug of milk;
If you're still praying to
A god packed in spice and parables,
Pinup for the romance of pain—

Well, I'm no corn farmer, no
Thin grin in a seersucker suit, not even
A cockroach crawling out from under
The broken bottom of the apocalypse. I could
Dispose of the guilty print, erase
The dark erratic residue of words,
Recto and verso; I could
Fill in this flyleaf, this slip of emptiness,
With a twisted script
Lying in state on the endsheet. But what
Would that press of letters prove? It's only
One more false measure to
Avoid the void—a voice
Patched over the static, glazing
The page with its own late name.

Notes

"Ohio Haiku": The "good book" referred to in section 4 is Anne Imbrie's memoir, *Spoken in Darkness.*

"Mardi Gras Indians": Background information was drawn from Jason Berry, Jonathan Foose, and Tad Jones's book, *Up from the Cradle of Jazz: New Orleans Music since World War II.*

"Grand Isle": Part of this poem is based on Sally Kittredge Evans's brief history of Grand Isle.

"Evening Services on North Rampart Street": Many details in this poem were suggested by Michael P. Smith's *Spirit World.*

"Storyville": This sequence draws on information from four books: Al Rose's *Storyville, New Orleans;* Lee Friedlander's *E. J. Bellocq: Storyville Portraits;* Alan Lomax's *Mister Jelly Roll;* and Robert Tallant's *Voodoo in New Orleans.* I am also grateful to Wilbur E. Meneray, Head of Rare Books and Manuscripts at Tulane University's Howard-Tilton Memorial Library, where I conducted research in the Al Rose Collection and the William Hogan Archive of New Orleans Jazz.

"Pilgrimage": William Faulkner Rushton's *The Cajuns: From Acadia to Louisiana* first led me to Fred's Lounge, and it also supplied some details for this poem.

"On My Mother's Death": In the second stanza, I have used a phrase taken from my mother on her deathbed. In those last days, she spent most of her time staring into space. Once, when asked what she was looking at, she answered, "The bare blank."

Other Books in the Crab Orchard Award Series in Poetry

Muse
Susan Aizenberg

This Country of Mothers
Julianna Baggott

White Summer
Joelle Biele

In Search of the Great Dead
Richard Cecil

Names above Houses
Oliver de la Paz

The Star-Spangled Banner
Denise Duhamel

Winter Amnesties
Elton Glaser

Fabulae
Joy Katz

Train to Agra
Vandana Khanna

Crossroads and Unholy Water
Marilene Phipps

Misery Prefigured
J. Allyn Rosser

Becoming Ebony
Patricia Jabbeh Wesley